YOUR KNOWLEDGE HAS VALUE

- We will publish your bachelor's and master's thesis, essays and papers

- Your own eBook and book - sold worldwide in all relevant shops

- Earn money with each sale

Upload your text at www.GRIN.com
and publish for free

Bibliographic information published by the German National Library:

The German National Library lists this publication in the National Bibliography; detailed bibliographic data are available on the Internet at http://dnb.dnb.de .

This book is copyright material and must not be copied, reproduced, transferred, distributed, leased, licensed or publicly performed or used in any way except as specifically permitted in writing by the publishers, as allowed under the terms and conditions under which it was purchased or as strictly permitted by applicable copyright law. Any unauthorized distribution or use of this text may be a direct infringement of the author s and publisher s rights and those responsible may be liable in law accordingly.

Imprint:

Copyright © 2018 GRIN Verlag
Print and binding: Books on Demand GmbH, Norderstedt Germany
ISBN: 9783668780538

This book at GRIN:

https://www.grin.com/document/432905

Veny Ari Sejati

Introduction to Journalism

GRIN Verlag

GRIN - Your knowledge has value

Since its foundation in 1998, GRIN has specialized in publishing academic texts by students, college teachers and other academics as e-book and printed book. The website www.grin.com is an ideal platform for presenting term papers, final papers, scientific essays, dissertations and specialist books.

Visit us on the internet:

http://www.grin.com/

http://www.facebook.com/grincom

http://www.twitter.com/grin_com

Veny Ari Sejati

Introduction to Journalism

For:

Raya Suko & Tata Suko

Contents

Preface and Acknowledgments

About the Author

PART 1. JOURNALISM

Understanding Journalism

Medium Journalism

What is Journalism Language

Summary

Review Questions

PART 2. PRESS

Understanding the Press

Visual Press Elements

Summary

Review Questions

PART 3. NEWS

What is News?

Straight News

Feature

News Variety

News Construction

News Elements

News Search Techniques

News framing

Summary

Review Questions

PART 4. INTERVIEW

What is Interview?

Interview guidelines

What is Off the Record?

Conventional Ethics

Statistics Interpretation

Summary

Review Questions

References

Preface and Acknowledgments

I present this book to students as future journalists and future practitioners in various fields of work. Basically, the whole field of work requires the science and skills of journalism so that the audience, consumers, clients, feel interested and confident about what we serve through the writing and help us achieve the goal. Written communication using grammar based on rules journalism could avoid misunderstanding in communication. This book uses Jurnalistik, Pendekatan Teori dan Praktek by Asep Saeful Muhtadi as main reference and other books as supported references.

Special thanks go to my students, Suzuki Magetan, Grin Verlag, Annabel Reib, Daniel Olbrich, Patrick Hammer, chief editor of Radar Bojonegoro newspaper Anas Abdul G who assists journalistic guidance on my journalism work, in particular Suko Puji Laksono, great lecturers in Program Studi Komunikasi Universitas Merdeka Madiun: Maria Magdalena Widiantari, Nunik Hariyani, Fikri Hassan. Kindness & warmth of my families: Sutono's family and Sumiyanto's family. They have always supported my work in ways.

May be useful

PART 1. JOURNALISM

The purpose of this part:
1. Students as future journalists are able to describe the definition of journalism, the medium of journalism, and what is the language of journalism?
2. Students as future journalists could make examples or cases from discussion part 1

Understanding Journalism

The practice of news delivery has been around since few years ago, for example in Indonesia there was kentongan used as a tool for sending news. The different sound of kentongan is a sign, depending on the delivered news, whether the news of grief, theft, flood, etc. The alerts meant the messages delivered to the public were not to be confused with other messages. With the development of tapping and science, the current delivery of news to the public using notes in the form of journalism activities.

Journalism according to Carey (1989) is a form of communication to transmit information to the public (Plapper, 2007). Journalism means daily. The word journal comes from French: journal is diary. Therefore, etymologically, journalism is a work of art in terms of making notes about everyday events, works of beauty that could attract the attention of audiences so that it could be enjoyed and utilized for the necessities of life. Journalism is an attempt to get everyone to know what is unknown. Messages about events / events occur every day that is processed into news and presented to the public is journalism. Journalism by Weiner (1990) in Ana Nadya Abrar (2005) is the whole process of collecting facts of writing, editing, and broadcasting news (Mulyadi, Nadi & Asti Musman, 2013).

Journalism could also be derived from the term diurnarius or diurnarii meaning people who seek and cultivate (quote and reproduce) information to be sold to anyone in need. Understanding journalism is the skill or artwork of journalists, in the sense of seeking (information), selecting and collecting (news material), and process (arrange) news script to meet the needs of audiences (Suhandang, 2010). According to Dahlgren (2001), thereby, journalistic work is to report stories that tell accurately and impartially about reality that exits independently from these stories and outside of the journalistic institutions (Plapper, 2007). The process of journalism is to seek, collect, select, and process information containing news value, and presents to the audience through periodic mass media, both print and electronic (Rohmadi, 2011).

Principles of journalism include: journalistic truth or the process of collecting and verifying data. Journalists deliver meaning in a fair and reliable and transparent report; loyalty to society means journalists provide news without fear and favor and maintain community loyalty and public interest; discipline to verify by looking for witnesses, sources, to be objective; have freedom from the source of freedom of the soul and thought are : an honest source, has the ability to deliver information and do not loyal to a particular group; serving as a free observer of power and emphasizing the importance of being a watchdog; provide forum for comments and criticism from the public; trying to make the important thing interesting and relevant; keeping the news proportional and comprehensive; have a sense of ethics and responsibility as a moral compass.

We need to know the variety of journalism around us (Mulyadi, Nadi & Asti Musman, 2013) for example: **journalism audiences** could be seen from segmentation, whether women, men, children. Differences of audience would be different Language used; **ideological journalism** is a journalism that does not care about who the audience is, but emphasizes the ideology or vision of the mission; **participatory journalism** is undertaken at the initiative of a society that does not have a journalist profession, participatory journalism is valued because the media generally prefer to dramatize events and the media is often caught up in the doctrine of "names make news"; **literary journalism** is a writing that combines reportage and literary style writing so as to attract the attention of audiences; **investigative journalism** has elements: exposing a crime in the public interest or other harmful actions, widespread case scale, answering all important questions, exposing the actor and evidence, the public could understand the complexity of the reported problem and be able to make a decision or changes based on that report. Investigation into journalism would be committed to flesh out appropriations of law, justice, accountability, transparency, and democracy; **prophetic journalism** is a form of journalism that provides clues to change based on ethical and prophetic moral ideals and ideals based on ethics, e.g. secular news; **corporate journalism** preaches the work culture of the company or relates to events in the company; **partisan journalism** takes sides with certain parties, such as admiring and giving a lot of praise to certain parties; **journalism multicultural** perspective has multiculturalism and pluralism used to view the reality to be constructed, processed into news. through multiculturalism journalism would create harmonious society, peace, tolerance; **peace journalism** about the benefits of violence in a conflict and the wisdom of conflict, and its coverage is people oriented. Journalism is more concerned with empathic victims of conflict than the conflict process; journalists in **disaster journalism** are thinking about how to get to the disaster site, conduct interviews, and get exclusive pictures or videos. However, it often results in the loss of humanitarian instinct of journalists; **yellow journalism** is exploiting something to grab the attention and interest of audiences evoke emotions without being given the facts. Headline titles and news content presented in excessive even tend to make controversy, especially on pictures or video. **Multimedia journalism** distributes and presents information through the computer by utilizing sound, animation, video, text, images, etc. Linear multimedia e.g. television, active and linear content, the process of delivering information without navigation controls to the audience. Non-linear multimedia e.g. computer games, offering user interactivity in controlling the process of delivering information; **online journalism** is the process of delivering information using internet media; **independent journalism** is an impartial process of preaching to the group or a certain group (cover both side), so that the public gets correct information so as not to form sentiment on the community; **political journalism** according to Russert and Kovach (2001) is aimed at placing the interests of the ruling party in order to remain correlated and responsible answer to public interest and explain to voters how to relate expectations when exercising their rights as citizens and what to do by the government. **Journalism ngejazz** is the knowledge of journalism on the sensation of a trend in society with light and popular language; **adversary journalism** is journalism in opposition to government; **journalism checkbooks** is journalism that always provides a high cost to pay for the source; **alcohol journalism** is a journalism that emphasizes news content; **crusade journalism** is a journalism that has a mission to achieve group goals; **journalism of communism-etatism** i.e. kamerad journalism means all friends if they are friends and enemies if they are enemies; **Islamic journalism** almost similar to crusade journalism but based on the tradition of Islamic preaching; **liberal journalism** refers to US democracy.

Medium Journalism

Mass media has functions such as **broadcasting information** as its main function because the community uses mass media to meet information needs; presenting a message of knowledge is an **educational function**; and **entertaining**, presents a message of entertainment that aims to offset hard news; and influencing functions play an important role in people's lives. The role of the mass media becomes important because of the wide coverage in disseminating information, multiplier of message, media could make the discourse of a political event according to their respective views, and the agenda setting function owned by the mass media (Rohmadi, 2011). According to Dye and Zeigler, the main function of mass media is news making, mass media observes and reports events; interpretation, the media would analyze and assess the events; socialization, the mass media seeks to indoctrinate the audience in connection with the prevailing values; persuasion, mass media would seek to influence audiences; and agenda setting, the mass media determines anything related to important issues, defines the problem, and submitted trouble shooting suggestions.

Writing news in print and electronic media is the process of uncovering the facts in writing, then printed and published in print media or electronic media broadcast. Print and electronic media have different characters and properties so complement each other. According to Baschwitz (1946) and Wahyudi (1986), publicity means could be disseminated to the public; universality which means the content of the message is general, could be read, heard, seen by anyone; periodicity, could be presented to audiences periodically or permanently, continuity means news which broadcast on an ongoing basis until the news is no longer considered important and interesting.

Mass media and electronic media use different approaches to the messaging strategy which would be delivered to audiences, depending on the characteristics of the media itself. On electronic media, the message received by audiences only a glance, the audience must always be in front of electronic media. The broadcast message is arranged in a formulation that is easily accepted by the audience by using simple language and logic so easily understood when the message is received. Messages which difficult to understand by the public could not be repeated because changed other messages. Electronic media has low persuasion power. Messages delivered could be consumed by everyone including the illiterate. The writing of electronic media texts is directed to a plurality of audiences, for the writer in print media should be able to capture the interest and imagination of the audience, words and pictures have a purpose, understand the interest and attention of the audience. Even script writers on radio should be able to create written illustrations and construct a picture of facts, sound effects, music, and dialogue. Writing on radio is specific and able to make the atmosphere into the form of sound and dialogue. The writer on the television should be able to consider what the program looks like, how long the broadcast produces for each show, etc. The factors that should be considered in determining the quality of television news according to Soewardi Idris (1987) is to use the **language of short and simple news**, directly addressed to the audience, not using foreign terms, avoid inverted sentence; **news movie** is the main element makes the news interesting and alive. Silent film is equipped with a script containing an explanation of the event in accordance with the series of movies that would be read by readers, while sound on film is not equipped with sounds and words that explain the contents of the movie because it is recorded automatically. Cameramen on silent films and sound on films are required to record events and be used to edit movies and to compile the completeness of the manuscripts and comments; **news scripting movie** should be previewed so as not soon forgotten by audiences. Scriptwriting is done in the following ways: first, synchronized scripting, i.e. matching text and drawings, usually used for writing long live news scripts and depicting dramatic acts or deeds. Second, the way blocked scripting is the way without matching posts and images, the script only describes the background behind events and information in general.

In the print media, messages received by the audience could be reviewed and studied and saved for reading back every time. Messages are organized more sophisticated, scientific, in higher Language and logic, the reader could grasp the message slowly. Magazines could reveal events which the newspaper does not reveal in depth although unpublished every day. Print media is still in demand by the community because every medium has different characteristics. Print media news writing using 5W +1H formulas (who, what, when, where, why, and how). The formulation is a reference for authors to write interesting and interested public audiences. Magazine news articles highlight the selection of the information section, the overall content of the news by emphasizing the question of why and how. On the investigation news why and how are not revealed newspaper news. In the headline, the journalist must make sure that the headline should include the 5W+1H formulation answer, since the headline should help audiences who do not have much time to deal with the media.

What is Journalism Language

The language of journalism is a mass communication language that has short, dense, simple, attractive, smooth, clear, democratic, populist, logical, grammatical, avoids informal and foreign sentences, precise diction, denotes use of active sentences, avoids technical word and obedient to ethics. According to Kurniawan (1997) the language of journalism is the language used by journalists in writing journalism, such as newspapers, magazines, tabloids, bulletins, etc. (Rohmadi, 2011). The language of journalism should be short, solid, straightforward, interesting, fluent, and clear, and obey the rules, the social norms that have been determined.

The language of journalism has a characteristic than scientific language because it has different characters based on the type of writing to be published. The language for writing investigative reportage is more thorough than Language to write features. The language for writing headline is different from Language for feature writing. Speaking in written and spoken language should avoid ambiguous because it could lead to misunderstandings and cause disputes.

Writing news must use careful language to avoid ambiguity and other errors. In frequent journal deviations or language errors include: **morphological aberrations** often occur in titles that use active sentences, i.e. the use of a prefix or prefix verb is omitted; **syntax errors** in the form of grammatical errors or sentence structure caused by bad logic; **vocabulary errors** are often done for reasons of euphemism or minimizing the adverse effects of news; **spelling mistakes** are often found in print and often unintentionally; **beheading errors** generally caused by computer programs using English.

The use of good journalism language is seen from a good paragraph arrangement, meaning that the development of the paragraph must be complete and show unity in its content. Paragraphs become imperfect because insertion is not related to the topic sentence or main idea. For that the author must remark to the linkage of pronouns and parallel ideas written in sentence parallel.

Summary

Journalism is a form of communication to transmit information to the public. Understanding journalism is the skill or artwork of journalists, in the sense of seeking (information), selecting and collecting (news material), and process (arrange) news script to meet the needs of audiences. Mass media has functions such as broadcasting information, educational function; and entertaining. Writing news in print and electronic media is the process of uncovering the facts in writing, then printed and published in print media or electronic media broadcast.

The language of journalism is a mass communication language that has short, dense, simple, attractive, smooth, clear, democratic, populist, logical, grammatical, avoids informal and foreign sentences, precise diction, denotes use of active sentences, avoids technical word and obedient to ethics.

Review Questions

1. Describe the definition of journalism!
2. Mention the function of mass media. Then make examples of programs on electronic media or news on the print media on each function.
3. Find an article in print. Then analyze the Language in the article. Is there a Language error / deviation? If so, explain!

PART 2. PRESS

The purpose of this chapter:
1. Students as future journalists are able to explain the definition of the press and the elements of the visual press.
2. Students as future journalists could make examples or cases from discussion part. 2.

Understanding the Press

Many people say the press as journalism or journalism is the press, even more familiar the term press than journalism. The press refers to broadcasting equipment, derived from the word press, meaning printing or printing press, where the printing press is used to publish newspapers. Press means printing, printed publications. There are two general definition of the press, the narrow sense, namely the newspaper; both of which are broadly defined, i.e. community institutions that run journalism activities. The press first was limited to publications in print, but now the broader sense of the press includes electronic media and publishing. John C. Merril (1991) reveals that the press is seen as a force capable of affecting society. The press is the content of human interaction and the expression of various kinds of think, events, and all the problems which following.

The press has a close relationship to journalism, the press as a medium of mass communication media would not be useful if the message presented away from the principles of journalism. The work of journalism would also not be useful if it is not delivered by the press as the medium. The press is one of the social powers that exercise free and responsible control both for society and for other social forces. There are five prerequisites for a free and accountable press to the public according to the Hutchins Commission (Mulyadi, Nadi & Asti Musman, 2013) : the media must present a credible, complete, intelligent daily event in a meaningful context, the media should serve as a forum for commentary exchange and criticism, the media must project a picture that truly represents the constituent group in society, the media must present and explain the goals and values of society, the media must provide full access to the hidden information one day.

The purpose of the press (Muhtadi, 1999) are for the reader to know the news; change public behavior through ideas in editorial, interpretative reporting, etc. Editorial and interpretative reporting could influence the reader because the writing is positive subjective for the benefit of society; improve the intellectual quality of the reader directly or indirectly.

According to Schramm (1954), in the life of society, the press has an informative and interpretative function of events occurring in life, as an instrument of everyday life, as an entertainer, a tool for maintaining social prestige, and as an inner liaison understanding to sustain life where moral size continues to grow. Function the press according to Hout (1947) are education, illumination, and commentary (Suhandang, 2010). **Education function**. Media is an effective channel for social, political, moral, and other massive means of life. In playing the function, the mass media in particular presents the space of science to increase the knowledge of the audience. The function of education is to emphasize, because the audience would already have the preparation to receive the broadcast. The press disseminates knowledge about progress in the field of life and audiences would evolve to the level of expected intelligence. Increasing knowledge, then the audience feel the addition of the necessities of life. The press is considered very important inside increase knowledge. The press serves the needs of society for information. Because people have a lot of information needs, the press always try to present something related to life. Audiences need to be informed of everything on earth as the occurrence of major events, the social realities, the ideas and the minds of people being the talker, the hot issue, etc. **The function of information** is information includes news, information or additional description of general events that are absolutely necessary to know the public. According to Rochady (1970) the press as a function of lighting is divided into four kinds of work: educational work, interconnection human, helping to shape public opinion, and as a control tool that could prevent unexpected things (Suhandang,

2010). **The function of comments** is a response and assessment of an event that the news is published in the mass media. An event is often a conversation of people and a press concern, so it would be broadcast in the form of news, responses, and comments.

In addition to the above, the work and function of the press is to realize human communication with other human beings in order to survive (Mulyadi, Nadi & Asti Musman, 2013). Informative function is giving information or news to the general public in a regular way; the control function is telling what works well and or unwell; an interpretive or directive function i.e. provide interpretation and guidance to the community; entertaining function is telling a funny story even though it is not important news; the function of guarding the right of the citizens in the form of guarding and securing private rights; the economic function is serving the economic system through advertising; self-help function is the press has an obligation to cultivate the ability to be unaffected from financial problems.

Visual Press Elements

Journalists are people on duty, formal or informal, searching-gathering and processing news material into draft news, commentary and advertisements that are broadcasted. Journalists are people who have visual acuity and hearing in search of news. The main work of journalists is to seek, collect, analyze facts and events in society, then inform to the audience. Journalists must be professional and have extensive knowledge because they face challenges in the field; should be able to explore, search, analyze all facts and news from the public; must be able to harmonize and balance opinions that appear in a plural society. Journalists work as the impulse of his conscience as a profession and bounding by code of ethics and criteria. Code of ethics is the norm that binds the occupation, while the criteria is a selection tool to enter a profession. Professional discipline binds members who have joined the profession. Journalists are not only worked with looking for news but also playing a role in compiling news to be published.

These days, most of the press is not truthful, honest, competent, disciplined, virtuous, diligent, upright, and political neutral (Robert, Odey Simon&Eric Ndoma Besong, 2017). For that journalist must have ethics such as: exploring news in an ethical way, respecting the right of source, making quotation correctly; not taking money; consistent on balanced principles and objectivity (Mulyadi, Nadi & Asti Musman, 2013). Ethics ensure objective journalism, grounded by truth, fairness, honesty, decorum, moral uprightness, sincerity and generally accepted standards, norms and values; ethics prevail on journalists to practice at all times their professional norms, rather than compromising them for unusual, for the good interest of all; ethics act as a watchdog over the journalists for which they are bound to cut their excesses; ethics shape the worldview, perception, relationship and deeds of the journalists; ethics spell out the core responsibilities of the journalists, for which they often try to discharge if and where possible completely (Robert, Odey Simon&Eric Ndoma Besong, 2017).

In detail explained that the main works, vision, mission of journalists are: seeking, collecting, analyzing, and presenting facts and events in society; able to align and inform events proportionally; impartial one race, tribe, class, or political party; able to provide information enlightenment to the public so as to bring progress to society and nation; participate in the intellectual life of the nation and state through writings, critical news analysis, and innovative.

Journalists are divided into two. First, the journalist in charge of finding and collecting information or news material through coverage of events that occur. Journalists have a high curiosity about an event. Groups of journalists are important people who know what is called news, how to get, where get news sources. Morally, a journalist knows the principles of right and wrong and realizes that he is responsible for informing the news correctly. In a media company there are usually some journalists who only writes a story about an event or a field, such as a political field only. When in a location there are important events outside the field, the journalist would contact the editor manager to see if there is already covering the event. In making news, journalists use the guidelines "who, what, when, where, why, how" especially if at an unplanned time.

All journalist work under mastery of editors. There are three terms editors: beat man, leg man, correspondent. **Beat man** is in charge of covering news related to officials, such as covering police stations, courts, etc. While the leg man is in charge of covering certain events based on the desk, for example within a day of investigating, afterwards reporting the speech, etc. **Leg man** works only on obtaining facts or data only while news writing submitted to each desk. **Correspondent** is a journalist who lives in an area and is in charge of covering events that occur in their respective areas, then report to the editor. Correspondents are journalists stationed in other countries or regions, outside the central office area (Rohmadi, 2011). **Out-of-town correspondents** provide news about areas far from their media offices but are still areas where the broadcast is in circulation, in collaboration with legs, paid for by the space containing the news, often serving two or more mass media. **The foreign correspondent** is in charge of covering overseas news to be sent to the local media office, must have special skills and master works. He must be able to explain the existing situation abroad so that the audience understands the events reported. Foreign correspondents must have local language proficiency. Salary earned higher than other correspondents because in delivering the news requires a high cost. **War correspondents** should be carried out by people who have the ability, are in charge of covering the war, using light fixtures. **The binagraha correspondent** is a special journalist worked with covering events at the office of the President of the Republic of Indonesia, covering the activities of the president by attending press conferences with the president and ministers. Binagraha is the world's largest news center and many newspapers send correspondent there. **Informal journalists** are not bound by certain media, such as public relations in charge of making press releases. In addition, there are also freelance journalists who seek news materials, process, compile and then submitted to the mass media who want to receive their news. The editor would check the truth of the news from an unknown correspondent.

Second, **editor** is in charge of editing and revising articles coming from the author, works with editing and selecting news before printing, working teamwork.

The main work of the editor is how to make the news public, interesting to read, and there is no error news. In addition, the editor also refines the news script. Someone could not have said to be a good editor if does not understand what the news is and what it means for the success of the publication. If there is an extraordinary event, then the editor discards the news which considered less valuable. Technically there are two editor jobs: read, revise, and re-arrange the news script received. The editor must be thorough, have a good job history, analytical thinking, could visualize, have knowledge about the process of mechanization of mass media production, must be healthy and strong.

In order to work, journalists must have standard of journalist competence agreed, including: **awareness** of ethical and legal awareness in order to avoid mistakes such as plagiarism and bribery, journalistic sensitivity in order to reveals information that could be developed into journalism, networking and lobbying to obtain an honest and accurate source; **knowledge** is general knowledge covers problems in various fields, special knowledge related to field coverage, knowledge of theory and principle of journalism includes knowledge of the theory and principles of journalism and communication; **skill** in the form of reporting to find, to get, to have, to save, to process, to deliver information, skill use tool and information technology to support its profession, research skill and investigation that is using reference sources, data, tracking, and verifying information, analytics and reporting skills include the ability to collect, read and filter facts and then search relationship of facts and data.

All manuscripts written by journalists are submitted to **publishers**, or publishers assign journalists to write good, interesting, and profitable events. Publishers try to make the manuscript could be presented through printed media to be submitted to the audience and are in demand by them. Publishers have the work of editing, production, and distribution, and circulation. The publisher is the person or institution that conducts the business of publication through the management policy. Publication is an activity to make public know. Publishers work with journalists, photographers, journalists, illustrators. Distribution is also noticed by publishers, such as stores, gathering retailers and newspaper deliveryman.

Printing is a work unit in which the news script would be printed, forming letters and drawings, displaying knowledge to be readable by the public. Based on how it works, printing has three basic methods of **relief** where the ink is applied to a medium material in a printing process, **Plano graphically** is the ink in a plate covering the surface of the material being in the printing process, and **the intaglio** is the ink melted from the underside of the material in the printing process.

Summary

The press refers to broadcasting equipment, derived from the word press, meaning printing or printing press, where the printing press is used to publish newspapers. Press means printing, printed publications. The purpose of the press is for the reader to know the news; change public behavior through ideas in editorial, interpretative reporting, etc. Function the press are education, illumination, and commentary. Visual Press Elements are: 1). Journalists are people on duty, formal or informal, searching-gathering and processing news material into draft news, commentary and advertisements that are broadcasted. All manuscripts written by journalists are submitted to publishers. 2). The publisher is the person or institution that conducts the business of publication through the management policy. 3). Printing is a work unit in which the news script would be printed, forming letters and drawings, displaying knowledge to be readable by the public.

Review Questions

1. Describe what is the press!
2. Explain the functions of the press?
3. Describe the elements of the visual press!

PART 3. NEWS

The purpose of this chapter:
1. Students as future Journalists are able to explain what is news, straight news, feature, news variety, news construction, news element, view, news search techniques, news framing.
2. Students as future journalists could make examples or cases of discussion from part. 3.

What is News?

All the newspaper sheets were filled with news. News is the substance of the mass media and is considered merchandise marketed by media companies. All events and opportunities become news. All new things are information that can be conveyed to others in the form of news. Geographical factors, traditions, beliefs play a role in determining the news. Media companies present media with different nuances. news created and aired for public interest. According to Dr. Williard G.Bleyer in Wonohito (1960), news is everything that is actual and attracts the attention of a number of readers, and the best news is the news that draws the most attention to the large number of readers (Suhandang, 2010). News is information on events broadcast to others, the events that are delivered are usually unique and interesting events (Rohmadi, 2011). News is a report or notice about any actual event that attracts public attention, bringing something fresh. News is something that has never happened, something that could be considered different for different people or communities as well. News is the main ingredient of mass media, electronic and print. The nature of the news is to provide information quickly to the public, if news quickly received public then the news will quickly spread. In writing the news should take notice to the specific writings, the sentence should be short, vary the sentence, the alenia should be short, avoid the numbers at the beginning of the sentence, mention the identity of the people, avoid trademarks, use quotes, throw away unimportant words, avoid foreign terms.

Print media have different considerations in determining news placement based on importance of news. Some consideration of whether the news is interesting or not, whether the news is a report of new events, facts or opinions; does the news provide information about something the public has never known before?; whether the news caught the attention of the entire audience; whether news adds to the audience's knowledge of what really happened. Feasible or unfeasible the source of the news needs to be considered the actual and factual elements. Actual means relevant, warm, high news value. While factual means news based on reality, fact, and not subjective.

News based on the nature of the occurrence is **the expected news** or news about events that have been previously expected to occur. Journalists usually already know the number of people attending, the form of the event, etc. **Unexpected news**, i.e. news of a totally unexpected event, a sudden occurrence of events, so journalists often find out through news sources who know the event, such as an earthquake. As for news, based on the content of the problem there is **religious news** which describes the life of religion, religious fanaticism, because it attracts the reader's attention; education news concerning education issues as a whole; **news science or scientific news** is the news involves the advancement of science in the form of new invention, new concept or theory, scientific research result, etc. In general, the community is not interested in the news of science but some people are interested in the progress of science-related; **political news** concerning political events in general both in formal and non-formal institutions. Politics concerning human interest and most societies involved in political activities; **economic news** is one of the public interest, so the mass media provides a special page of the economy. In the print media, generally economic news is presented as a headline; **legal and court news** is also interesting and in demand by the public. The whole mass media presents the news because the law is something basic to humans and could be used as a lesson for humans; **crime news** catches people's attention, how the crime happened so that it could be a lesson do not to become the perpetrator crime and crime victims. Authors of crime news should avoid the alleged accusations and allegations of right wrong; **sports news** to attract the attention of audiences because in sport events there are elements of conflict who wins and who lost. Media companies generally have sports journalists. The journalist must have the attention and pleasure in the sport, knowing the rules of the game, the game system, the terms used in the sport; **human news and events** are news related to various events. The media rarely covers the news because the events are often unexpected. Usually, the news is written by journalists who daily have other work such as religion, sports, etc.; **world news and women,** the theme of women is very interesting and never exhausted to be a topic of conversation, for example emancipation, female labor, etc. Print media, Newspaper and magazine even specifically reveal women's issues, such as Kartini magazine, women's tabloids, etc.

So that the news is interesting, the facts are organized into a unity that explains each other in the form of short writing and able to reveal the facts desired audience. The aspects in organizing news (Muhtadi, 1999) are objectivity and structure of the story. Writing facts from an objective point of view, the source should be written using a by line pattern, the writer or journalist is listed between the title and the news; besides, **objectivity** means does not add personal opinion in the news. **The structure of the story** in writing the news must present facts in sequence, in natural order, to the point, directly reveal the most interesting information to the unattractive information, the writing technique is made in the inverted pyramid format.

Straight News

Straight news serves people who do not have the free time to use the mass media. Audience just wants to know the main facts of an event without wanting to know unimportant things. News is made to convey an event that should be known to the public as soon as possible. The straight news product is **the matter of fact news** raises the main facts involved in the event; **action news** suggests actions, actions (events) involved in the event only or simply tells the event; **quote news** put forward a quote from what is revealed by the figures involved the event. Writing straight news uses inverted pyramid, written for what it is, and briefly.

Three straight news products if combined it would be a description tells and explains the events occur, could attract the attention of the audience, and answer the curiosity. Straight news usually only load or express facts as they are though sometimes added interpretation of the author if the fact presented has not provided a clear picture.

Feature

Feature could be interpreted as articles or special news or highlighted to be able to attract attention and enjoyed by audiences, the goal is fun and inform the audience. Characteristic feature is the human interest and there is a literary element. On features, events are often expired, less important, trivial, but want special attention. Feature conveys information in a special style and builds facts and one of the strategies used by print media to compete with electronic media, as well as often subjectively and emphasizes the occurrence of empathy. Authors have freedom in expressing opinions, tend to be subjective compared straight news, for that feature does not have to use a complete 5W + 1H. The nature of the feature is a form of writing made by the author based on personal opinions or ideas about a particular problem. the purpose of writing a feature is to express the idea of a particular problem, to provide problem solving, entertaining. The feature writing stage are :1). The background of the problem, 2). Identify the problem. 3). Description of the problem. 4). Conclusion. feature properties according to Mangiang is factual, explain the problem but not to be immediately reported, do not force opinion, article building is not bound inverted pyramid structure, un-necessarily answer 5W + 1H complete, timeless, feature lead written attractive short, single feature angle, narrow issue sphere (Mulyadi, Nadi & Asti Musman, 2013). Feature is arranged like inverted pyramid, consisting of head, lead, bridge between bridge and body, body, ending. Ending is used to restate the subject of the story by leaving a deep impression on the audience and describing a beautiful and clear story. As for the type of ending is the ending summarizes the description and lead to the lead, ending excitement that shock the audience, ending climax put forward the end of the story, and ending no settlement means not answer the main question.

Feature writing could be identified by looking at some things that are known as news stories, unknowing the term expired, more revealing the other side behind straight news, descriptive, humanist, light lead. Type of feature according to Ermanto (2005) is **human interest** or bright or called bride, presenting the problems of life, touching the human sense; **feature history**, raised interesting historical issues about historical events; **feature biography** or profile about life or the success of people admired by society; **travel feature** is a problem encountered on the way by journalists; **feature hint of doing something** teaches the audience to do something useful in everyday life; **scientific features** contain science presented simply, lively, and interesting. The others, there are a feature organization or project about the organization or company; **feature personal experience** contains the author's own experience or the experience of others written by the author; **feature introducing something** is a short article written to introduce something ; **feature popular scientific articles** telling a problem by using scientific sources in the form of books, research results, seminar papers, as a reference; **the history feature** reveals history without the author's interpretation and opinion; **feature interview** describes dialogue between journalists and others.

News feature is different from news feature. From the above explanation, news feature is not concerned with the element of time, but gives additional readings that are considered to remain actual even though events are not published as soon as possible. Feature news is also called interpretative news, emphasizing the purpose of news implicitly, giving the opportunity to the audience to interpret their own message in the news. Feature news will be more interesting if compiled using reportage style.

Forms news feature are **anti-feature** does not relate to time, news feature is an article about the problem being discussed, related to actual events and the development of straight news; **non-news feature** is essentially no related to news actuality, for example articles. In general, magazines use news feature because publish once a week or once a month.

Figure 1. Article

Image deleted due to copyright issues

News Variety

Spot news is a term for news that reports an event that must be immediately known by the audience; **talky news** is news that contains talks or speeches or interviews with someone; **trend news** is used for news that continues to grow in accordance with the continuation event; **depth news** for news obtained from exploring or self-written in depth, generally reporting the results of research or investigation of the author or journalist; **investigative news** conveying police or journalists' own tracking or investigation results developed based on research and investigation from various sources; **preview news** tells about a ceremony or particular activity; **interpretative news** developed from the opinion or assessment of journalists based on the findings of facts; **opinion news** is news about the opinions of people like scholars, experts, officials, etc.

Based on the subject matter area, there are various political news such as presidential election; economic news e.g. the formation of private banks; social culture news such as natural disasters; and security defense news such as war and crime. Based on the occurrence of events reported include regional or local, national, regional, and international news. Variety of news delivered based on the time of news coverage includes morning news, afternoon coverage, evening news, latest news.

News Construction

Headline is the essence of the news, written in one or two short sentences about the subject matter only. Headline usually called titles and have subtitles. Broadcast media accentuate the sounds on statements and print media to make the type, size, composition of letters, and words to attract audiences. Headline serves to call audiences to read, listen, watch news; helping the audience to know the events to be reported; provide graphics technical support to news. Audiences who do not have time to read through the news could get information through headline. The headline that occupies the top (usually the right) is called the top headline. Top headline means asking audiences to read first.

Based on the harmony deck, there are six headline forms:

1. Cross line headline consists of one deck, for example:

Minister of Fisheries Held Meetings with Fishermen

2. Pyramid headline has more than one deck and arranged like a pyramid, for example:

**Renovation of Presidential Palace of Bogor
before Meeting with the Southeast ASIA Country**

3. Inverted pyramid headline consist of several decks and arranged to form an inverted pyramid. Example:

**Toward Christmas and New Year
Police Standby 24 Hour**

4. Flush left headline consists of several decks arranged with a flat left edge, for example:

**Heavy Rain, Flood Hits Jakarta
The public is cautious**

5. Flush right headline consists of several decks and arranged with the right edge, for example:

**President of the Republic of Indonesia: Infrastructure
could be Enjoyed by the Community**

6. Hanging indention headline consists of three decks or more, the first deck is the longest deck, the next deck is the same length but shorter than the first deck, arranged as hanging on the first deck, for example:

Cheapest Down Payment and Installments
Enthusiastic consumers
Sales is Rising

There are seven headline based on typography:

1. Red in headline is an underlined headline, for example:

Company Leader: -------→ red in headline
Use of the Internet
Save the Budget

2. Rocket headline printed smaller and shorter and placed under or over a large and long headline. example:

Employees Request Increased Salaries and Other Benefits
Following the Government Regulation ----→ Rocket headline

3. Contrast headline uses different types and font sizes between decks, for example:

Following the Government Regulation
Employees Request Increased Salaries and Other Benefits

4. Big part mental headline is a contrast headline that printed thicker. Example:

Following the Government Regulation
Employees Request Increased Salaries and Other Benefits

5. Boxed headline is framed, for example:

> **Following the Government Regulation**
> **Employees Request Increased Salaries and Other Benefits**

6. Modified boxed headline is given a not full frame, for example:

Employees Ask for Incentive Increase

7. Jump headline is used as headings of news links placed on other pages, usually only the initial word of the original title, for example:

Title: **Employees Request Increased Salaries and Other Benefits**

(continue to page.12 columns 2-5)

Written:

Employee Request .... from page 1

Lead is the essence of the news; brief reports are climactic from the event report. Usually written in the first paragraph. Lead determines whether audiences are interested or not on the news. The lead answered 5W + 1H (what, who, when, where, why, + how) so that the audience immediately know the subject matter reported. **What lead** is to emphasize on the kind or form of events and begins by answering the question of what the events are preached, followed by other answers 5W + 1H. **Who lead** is when the lead or headline description the person involved in the news, for example: the perpetrator, the victim, the agency. Then lead starts from the person's name or institution. **When lead is** preceded by the event time followed by answering others 5W1H. **Where lead** emphasizes on the scene then followed by other answer of 5W + 1H. **How lead** is to explain how events are preached, emphasizing the continuity of events.

According to Bond (1961), based on the stylists of story composition there are eight forms of lead: **the digest lead** is composed by expressing all the important facts in a succinct and simple way; **the direct appeal lead** mimics the style of a personal letter to attract the attention of audiences, addressed directly to audiences using the word "you"; **the circumstantial lead** begins with an illustration of other conditions that are related to human interest events; **the statement lead** or the quotation lead begins with quotation marks or without using quotation marks, such as slogans, speeches, etc.; **the descriptive lead** depicts the scene or describe the state of the person involved in the reported event; **the suspended interest lead** provides interesting information and stimulate the audience to read through to completion;

preparation of **the tabulated lead** developed in the list or the table of each of the problems that appear in the reported event; **the various "stunts" lead** to the conclusion of events with other stunning and strange features, followed by chronological and detailed body stories.

In addition to the above mentioned, there are also **conjunction lead** beginning with conjunctions such as: "with", "when", etc.; **intuitive lead** starts with "for", etc.; **condition lead** begins with the word "if", etc.; **substantive lead** starts with the pronouns; **question lead** followed by a word or sentence followed by the answer; **astonisher lead** start with a surprising word or phrase; **the name lead** begins with the name of the person involved in the event. These lead is the same as who lead; **cartridge lead** begins with a tense or disturbing word or phrase.

The **news body** contains the completeness or detailed description of the unspecified news script on lead. News body is a news development. The provisions of the news body among others support and fulfill the 5W + 1H element, containing detailed descriptions, backgrounds, one alenia to the next alenia arranged continuously, one alenia consisting of one sentence or more but no more than thirty-five words, facts and background data that are commonly known to be indicated, 5W + 1H elements must be presented in the first three alenia, subtitle is used when switching topics. Information presented in the form of a description of the story by using a presentation style that could attract audiences. Presentation of the news body includes: pyramid-shaped, news body arranged in the form of a description of the story that begins with the things that are less important - important things - the most important thing.

Figure 2. body news in pyramid form

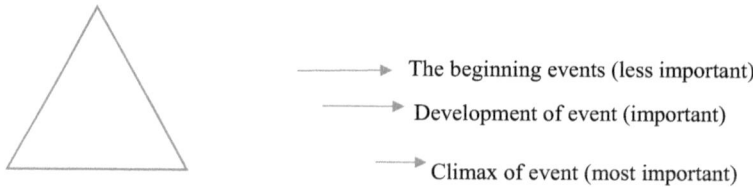

News body is **chronological**, almost the same as the pyramid form. The entire news body is built with the exposure of the beginning events and developed in accordance with the progress of the course of events. Generally used to notify in the form of action news or reportage.

The **inverted pyramid** news body is built by prioritizing the most important-important-unimportant. One of the reasons for using such structures is to help audiences who do not have much time to read the news, so that without a long time they could understand the main content of the news because the basic news is explained at the beginning of the news. The inverted pyramid structure provides ease in shortening long news, saving page space, facilitating news editing. If the place and time of presentation is impossible then unimportant information will not be used. Usually used to convey news is straight news especially matter of fact news. Inverted pyramid news writing is a writing technique that is tailored to the nature of the audience and the workings of journalists.

Figure 3. Body news shaped inverted pyramid

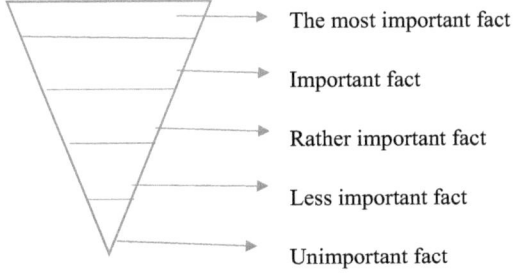

Events in the news body in the form of **block paragraph** is considered equally important, sorted according to what the author remembers in mind. Each issue puts forward in a single alenia so that each alenia has nothing to do with the next alenia. Construction of exposure does not indicate information that should be prioritized, all information of the same value and entitled to be known to the public.

Figure 4. Block paragraph chart

News Elements

The main character of news is to attract the attention of audiences. Attract events and presentations. For that, the main element of news is the general concern. the American Weekly states that the interests of audiences are a result, an endeavor, a culture, a belief, a tragedy, a health, a hero, a mystery, a self-improvement, a recreation, a romance, a science, and a security. According to Douglas Wood Miller there are three main elements of the news that could arouse the reader's interest of time, place, and content (Suhandang, 2010). Time must be actual. Audiences are generally interested in the place closest to where they live. The closer the scene occurs, the higher the audience interest to know. While news content that attracts audiences are a story about the personal reader, listener, and audience itself; stories about famous people and cities to audiences; stories of extraordinary things; famous names; the story of the match between two mutual forces opposite; stories of great or important events, stories of human interest; and animal stories.

News that has a high value will attract audiences to consume them. Factors for high-value news that are **timeliness**, generally people buy print media in the morning to get new and actual news. In general, the actual size is two days for daily media publication. Audience always wants to get new news. journalists must have high sensitivity associated with timeliness, such as whether the event is awaited by the community, what is going on, how to preach whether the feature or straight news.

Proximity, audiences are attracted to small event but near rather than important event but long distance. The closer the event is to the audience; the information will be preferred to the audience. Is the news relevant to the reader's residence? according to Tubbs and Moss (1991), proximity factors can tighten the communication process (Muhtadi, 1999). "The more closely two people are located geographically, the more likely they are to be attracted to one another". **Proximity** makes news different and interesting. **Size**, generally people are interested in something small or large; **importance**, the public enjoys news that fits their interests. In addition, there are elements that make the news has the attraction that is **self-interest.** News topics that have a close relationship with individual readers or listeners, the way, the style of exposure, will be preferred and can be exciting to attract attention. For the ability of writers in playing words and sentences can change audiences for example refuse to accept. The **conflict** in the news is uncovering the opposition that raises the attention of the audience. The upheaval can cause public attention. The theme of the conflict will be interesting if it adds community responses as supporters, experts, opponents. So the audience is easy in determining attitude. Consequence and impact is news reported by journalists to the public. What effect might the news have? The good news is the news has specific goals and targets, for whom the news, what changes are desired. The **human interest** on the news is more related to the content of the message, related to the unique and interesting nature of human life, can be written using straight news patterns, features, and editorial. Data can be obtained through coverage, investigation results, and interpretation of people.

View can be interpreted oral or written comments on an event, person, or opinion. In addition, view is a writing or speech in the form of comments and critical analysis of a problem, opinions of others, events, or circumstances and environmental conditions around. in journalism, view is a commentary on news or articles presented by the mass media to a phenomenon, events, and opinions that arise in the public environment. View coverage based on Sidney I Landau in Suhandang i.e. observation or inspection activities such as survey, inspection, etc..; wide view; findings; describes a scene; and opinions.

The **editorial** is an essay or actual comment on the mass media written by a special editor, containing a general view of the newspaper on important issues. Editorial is usually written by the chief editor or senior journalist in the print media. Editorial function is to explain the news, fill the background of the most important news, predict the future, give moral judgment on an event, condition or wisdom. Editorial features include an editorial opinion of the actual issue, containing a review of a problem, national and international news can be an editorial if it gives a national impact, editorial subjectivity. The author must convey good and true information, have broad insight, critical attitude, because editorial writing requires the sensitivity of the social situation and expected to provide criticism, suggestions, and solutions to various issues in the political, economic, social culture, etc. The editorial page is placed at the end of the news and closes with the author's pseudonym. Editorial writing structure is title, news explanation. The stages of writing an editorial are reporting (finding problems and collecting data by talking and by reading), reflection (selecting and classifying data from all sources), writing (compiling and presenting facts and data in editorial).

Column is a text about people's comments the problems that exist in the community. Columns can be interpreted a special essay on the mass media or form of writing in newspapers that specifically discusses certain news only. The person who created the column is called a columnist which means an author who contributed articles to the print media. Various columns are **humor column** containing critics in the form of humor; **gossip column** contains events that are being discussed. The eight columns according to Bond (1961) are editorial columns that are editorial-like but are based on one's opinion and appear using the byline, the standard column describes the less important uses of one or more paragraphs and often does not include the writer initials, the gado-gado column presents mixed writing, the contributor's column is done by amateurs about the good stuff and gets only publicity rewards, essay columns have unlimited but educational and non-boring issues, gossip columns presenting news about small town events with gossip writings, naturally written poems to attract audiences; corner, special articles; by line story; short stories, comics, etc. Writing columns can be done by everyone by searching topics, collecting written materials, written, edited, then sent to print. Column structure are the title, news peg, then opinion.

News Search Techniques

News hunting, news getting, or news gathering is one of the stages of news planning process, script writing process, and editing process of script. Techniques for finding news include: reportage, i.e. journalism activities covering directly to the scene with direct observation or indirect observation (based on source information). Interviews is FAQs between journalists and sources, conducted face to face or via phone, email, etc.; literature study is a technique of data collection through articles, papers, books, etc.; press conference is a statement submitted by a person to represent his or her institution concerning the image of the institution, supplemented with supporting data; press release is written by a person to represent his agency and for the benefit of the agency.

News framing

News framing is a technique used by journalists to create a discourse that will be captured by audiences, involving the selection of several aspects of social realist and making it stand out in a news. The technique used is to define the problem with consideration based on the value culturally applicable, diagnose the root of the problem by identifying the forces involved in the problem, making judgment is to provide a moral assessment of the root causes and effects, suggesting remedies that offer solutions with indicate the particular treatment and possible alleged effects (Mulyadi, Nadi & Asti Musman, 2013).

The type of news framing is media framing done by journalists who are influenced by social cognition, ideology, and social structure. Journalists should pay attention to news value, news framing, news worth when doing news framing; and individual framing done by audiences, is a mental state of the idea that guides individuals to process information. News section that can be used as news framing include: news headline, using empathy method; focus the news, using the association method of incorporating actual policy with news focus; cover the news, using the method of packing is to make the audience follow the invitation contained news.

Summary

News is everything that is actual and attracts the attention of a number of readers, and the best news is the news that draws the most attention to the large number of readers The nature of the news is to provide information quickly to the public, Characteristic feature is the human interest and there is a literary element. Feature conveys information in a special style and builds facts and one of the strategies used by print media to compete with electronic media, as well as often subjectively and emphasizes the occurrence of empathy. News Variety are spot news, talky news, news trend, depth news, investigative news, interpretative news, opinion news

Headline is usually called titles and have subtitles. Lead usually written in the first paragraph. The news body contains the completeness or detailed description of the unspecified news script on lead. Factors for high-value news are timeliness, Proximity, importance, self-interest, conflict, human interest.

View is a writing or speech in the form of comments and critical analysis of a problem, opinions of others, events, or circumstances and environmental conditions around. The editorial is an essay or actual comment on the mass media written by a special editor, containing a general view of the newspaper on important issues, usually written by the chief editor or senior journalist in the print media. Editorial functions are to explain the news, fill the background of the most important news, predict the future, give moral judgment on an event, condition or wisdom. Column is a text about people's comments about the problems that exist in the community. Columns can be interpreted a special essay on the mass media or form of writing in newspapers that specifically discusses certain news only. News hunting, news getting, or news gathering techniques for finding news include: reportage, interviews, literature study, press conference supplemented, press release is written by a person to represent his agency and for the benefit of the agency.

News framing is a technique used by journalists to create a discourse that will be captured by audiences, involving the selection of several aspects of social realist and making it stand out in a news.

Review Questions

1. Describe what is the news!

2. Look for an example of news opinion on print or electronic media, then give the reason why the news you call opinion news!

3. Make an example of cross line headline and pyramid headline!

4. Look for a headline in print (allowed online version), then analyze the headline form.

5. Look for a news in the mass media, then analyze news value and news search technique.

PART 4. INTERVIEW

The purpose of this chapter:
1. Students as future Journalists are able to describe what is an interview?, interview guidelines, what is off the record?, conventional ethics, statistical interpretation?.
2. Students as future journalists make examples or cases from the discussion of part 4.

What is Interview?

A technique to find data writing news is interview. Interview is a communication activity through the process of information exchange between journalist and news source. The source is the information window to open the facts to be reported. Journalists must be able to formulate the questions correctly and correctly, patient, confident, diligent, in order to dialogue and active interview. Interview is a way to search the news by face to face, using the phone media, internet, and email, between journalists and sources in certain places. A good interview is when the source tells you what they really think rather than thinking about what to say. The interview function is to collect news, data, facts, from someone as material to write interesting news. The purpose of the interview is to search information, test validity, confirm, get a direct greeting.

Various interviews according to Romli (2001) are: **news interview** is conducted to obtain information, confirmation, or source view of a problem or event that has been planned, often called information interview, for example about world soccer game; **personal interview** is used to obtain data about the personal and thoughts of people who have news value, the interview result is the person's profile; an **exclusive interview** conducted by someone or more journalists from one media specifically with sources related to a particular problem at an agreed place between journalists and sources; **casual interview** is done in no special way, incidentally, there is disagreement; **man in the street interview** by journalists by contacting various sources separately regarding a new situation or policy. The source of information is the public; **telephone interview** is an interview via telephone to a source who familiar to the journalist and usually done because of the urgent time; **question interview** is a written interview and the journalist conducted the interview because it has no way out of the problem. The advantage is the information obtained more clearly and easily understood, while the weakness is that journalists could not observe the attitude source when answering questions.

Interview guidelines

According to Bruce D. Itule (1991), to get news materials, mass media journalists do: **drafting guidelines and planning interviews** or guidelines after determining who will be interviewed. A good source is a resource that has the ability to speak, has knowledge of specific fields. Resources include scientists, bureaucrats, politicians, dissatisfied people, publicity seekers, public relations. After the guidelines have been completed, the journalist immediately makes an interview plan, based on experience or guidance as follows: 1). Make an appointment to determine the time and place of the interview. On writing feature and investigative news where deadline more flexible, journalist arrange schedule in advance for interview. In straight news, the journalist conducts an interview shortly when the event occurs. Interview planning helps journalists be more prepared and sources also have the opportunity to prepare the answers the journalists need. 2). Identify as a journalist and institution of work. Journalists introduce themselves to the source and origin of the mass media. The source is responsible for controlling the conversation. In the interview activities, avoid lies to avoid conflicts. 3). Consider the readiness of news sources, when, where, interview will be held. Journalists should allow the source to determine the time and place, since talk and more time are given to the source, the journalist just asks. If the source wants journalists choose time and place, then journalists should consider deadlines. 4). Explain the issues that will be asked for the source to know what the journalist wants, otherwise the source is aware of the competence to answer or reject, because the source has the right to refuse the interview if the topic is discussed beyond its competence. usually rejection is caused by wanting to take time for another job, worry to make mistakes, worry, want to protect others, do not know problems, feel embarrassed, traumatized. 6). Timely or interviewing as promised. Resources often do not serve well if the journalist is in time, because the source is the one who has the time. In addition, preparatory activities undertaken by journalists are preparing recorders and stationery; learn and master the problem; prepare questions well, specifically, importantly, and distinctively; prepare mentally, skill, and ability to conduct interview.

In an interview, a journalist should pay attention to the type of question and how to ask, the main structure and theme, the objectives to be achieved from the interview, record each answer quickly and accurately, have ethics when using the phone. There are two patterns of interview based on the subject matter and the type of person being interviewed: 1). Funnel interview, the interview pattern is arranged like funnel. This pattern is often used and relaxed because serious questions can be changed to the contrary. It usually starts with a background source question. The pattern is useful if news sources are not used to being interviewed before, the length of the interview is not pursued by deadlines or the news source has a lot of time, the need to start a general question about the background to establish communication closer so that the source is relaxed and open. 2). Inverted funnel interview, which is an interview pattern like an upturned chimney. Journalists ask the underlying issue without starting a general and light question, used for news sources who are used to being interviewed. So that the source is relaxed, frankly and openly when interviewed on a tough topic, the journalist must be able to choose the right time, empathy, feeling, sympathetic behavior, building personal relationships, do not showing book-notes or recorders. In disclosing personal issues, Bingham and Dillon (Muhtadi, 1999) provide practical guidance: preparing before the interview by knowing general problems first before asking specific problems, face to face interviews rather than on the phone to disclose personal issues, in casual setting so that the source feels relaxed, opens a rigid atmosphere with general questions, does not directly use the tape recorder before the source feel relaxed, the journalist gives an opportunity to the source to start talking without should be asked in advance, starting with the preface before asking, and persuading the news source politely if they do not want to comment. In addition, journalists should prepare notes that are easy to carry and use, able to write quickly but pay attention to face to face communication.

After the interview, journalist closes with the conclusion of reinforcement, praise, hope, thanks for the time given and appreciation, and asks how to contact the source if at any time need additional information. If any information is unclear, journalists will contact the source by telephone. There is no provision that before publication should be confirmed to the source, it avoids any revisions or edits made by the source.

What is Off the Record?

Off the record is literally a news source who does not want journalists to write and publish statements submitted, but only known by journalists and unknown by the public. Off the record also mean that journalists write and publish writing but do not mention the source name.

Off the record is often spoken especially by politicians to make the news seem important, but the public already knows. If the source asks off the record, the journalist could look for other sources who allow writing to be published. The source has the right and freedom to provide or does not to provide information. In the off the record information should be avoided direct quotations from the statement or opinion of a person because it is considered beneficial to the source or others. Quotes attract the attention and emotion of audiences, sources can communicate directly with audiences, generate emotions, animate news, invite readers' interest, etc. Quotation types include: **complete direct quotations**, all words and sentences are made equal to what the source discloses. The quotation is only used to reveal clear and specific statements, as well as describing descriptive statements for the audience to know the description of the source so that the audience as if through a dialogue with the source. The function of the quotation is as a supplement to reinforce facts and avoid the amount of attribution in the body of news; **partial quotations**, journalists quote only some of the most important sentences. Journalists usually change the word and take the whole sentence; **indirect or paraphrased quotations**, journalists could more freely formulate their own sentences to describe the message that the source discloses. The journalist concludes the source sentence using the journalist's own sentence but keeps mentioning the news source. Before the interview results are written with the above quotation, the journalist should pay attention to whether the source identity is mentioned or not, because sometimes the source asks not to be named.

Conventional Ethics

Before interviewing the source, the journalist should introduce himself and the origin of the media where he works, so that the source could self-control and realize that his words are news materials that may be published. **On the record** is that all data can be used as news material to be published, mention the name of source and identity. All source statements can be published. **Off the record** means that the information submitted by the source cannot be used as news material. If journalists want to publish news off the record, then they are looking for other sources that provide the same information and can be published. **On background** means that data can be used as news to be published but does not mention the name of the source. Caused source worry about leakage of information that is easy to trace. **On deep background** means data can be published using an indirect quote, the name of the source is not mentioned, for that journalists often try to find other sources that agree with the statement and write as a source of news. Information is only for journalists and tends to be exploited by officials.

Statistics Interpretation

Statistical data is generally presented in the form of tables, drawings, and numbers, arranged in the form of columns and lanes, so that information easily known. Through statistical data we know and compare the past, present, and possibly future events. However, not all journalists understand statistical data, even statistical data is considered boring. The task of journalists is to translate and expose the figures and images into a story that is easily understood by the audience. Through statistical data, journalists get news material quickly in a short time. Statistical data is used as complementary data and supporting news. The term statistics in journalism should be used appropriately because the misuse of the term will affect the interpretation of the audience. Such as percentages or percentage points indicate statistical difference, rupiah or number of population shows real difference. Journalists should use both terms to avoid misinterpretation.

The **life expectancy table** is a statistical information related to human life expectancy in a particular community. Journalists get information about the human age compared to tens of years ago, disease factors affecting life expectancy, etc. **Criminal reports** are usually reported by the police agency about the amount, form of harm caused by a crime. From these data explain the increase or decrease of crime rate from year by year, the form of crime, how long the change happened, etc. **College enrollment data** relating to education progress news. The mass media reported the news in the new school year. The data describes the increase and decrease of registrants from year by year, study programs that have increased and decreased, etc. **Data on smokers and drug users** explain the decrease and increase year by year, the highest and lowest smokers and drug user's area, etc. **National parks and zoos** is one of the cheap places of community entertainment, has the benefit of giving science to children. The tourism office makes statistical data about the community from which regions are most visited, how long visitors stay, etc. The **unemployment rate** is usually derived from the social service or the manpower service, in relation to employment and the labor force. The data describes the number or percentage of unemployment from year by year, the area where the highest number of unemployed, etc. **Public welfare reports or public services** explain the amount of funds used for the benefit of community welfare and public services sourced from the government and private. what is the magnitude if calculated per capita average, how much the overall fund from month by month or year by year, etc.? The average **data on the growth of forest protection** is very important in Indonesia because tropical forest is

Indonesia's natural wealth. Many people need forest protection information. what percentage of forest depreciation from time by time, how government efforts to tackle forest destruction, etc.? The **death rate by suicide** is an information that attracts the attention of audiences. The data explain how the average number of suicide deaths from year by year, the most sexes who die by suicide, etc. **Reports of legal bodies** such as cooperatives or other profit institutions are conducted periodically and openly in annual or mid-year, in relation to the assets owned. Information relates to the public interest in general so that it becomes important and interesting news. how much wealth they have for a certain time limit, what percentage of increase is gained from time by time, etc.

Summary

Journalists must be able to formulate the questions correctly, patient, confident, diligent, in order to dialogue and active interview. Interview is a way to search the news by face to face, using the phone media, internet, and email, between journalists and sources in certain places. In interview, journalists must be drafting guidelines and planning interviews, what will they do in an interview, and after the interview,

Conventional Ethics are on the record, off the record, on background, on deep background. Statistical data is generally presented in the form of tables, drawings, and numbers, arranged in the form of columns and lanes, so that information easily known. Through statistical data, journalists get news material quickly in a short time. Statistical data is used as complementary data and supporting news.

Review Questions

1. Mention the kinds of interviews.
2. Describe how the interview guides.
3. Look for quotes in a story. Then analyze the type of quotation.
4. Explain the conventional ethics in the interviews.
5. Look for news that describes statistical data. Then Analyze that data statistics news.

References

Muhtadi, A. S. (1999). *Jurnalistik. Pendekatan Teori dan Praktek.* Jakarta: Wacana Ilmu.

Mulyadi, Nadi & Asti Musman. (2013). *Jurnaslisme Dasae. Panduan praktis Jurnalis.* Yogyakarta: Citra Media.

Plapper, S. (2007). *E-journalism -How does electronic journalism differ from traditional journalism?* Munich: Grin Verlag.

Robert, Odey Simon&Eric Ndoma Besong. (2017). *Effect of Corruption and Bad Leadership on Journalism in Nigeria. Corruption and Bad Leadership, the Bane of Unethical and Subjective Journalism.* Munich: Grin Verlag.

Rohmadi, M. (2011). *Jurnalistik Media Cetak: Kiat sukses menjadi penulis dan wartawan profesional.* Surakarta: cakrawala media.

Suhandang, K. (2010). *Pengantar Jurnalistik. Seputar Organisasi, produk, & kode etik.* Bandung: NUANSA.

YOUR KNOWLEDGE HAS VALUE

- We will publish your bachelor's and master's thesis, essays and papers

- Your own eBook and book - sold worldwide in all relevant shops

- Earn money with each sale

Upload your text at www.GRIN.com and publish for free